S H E

Fully Hydrated

Gwyn RC Moses

Foreword by:

Sheila E. Battle

SHE, Fully Hydrated

Cover design: Mike Schrum

Images: istockphoto

ISBN: 978-1-952733-24-6

Library of Congress Cataloging-in-Publication Data

Foreword

SHE, Fully Hydrated…

I didn't know her, but somehow, I did. Our families were connected through love, marriage and faith, but She and I had never met. Once we did, everything about it was right, on time and Soul good. Our first face to face started with me sharing that I was writing a book. I was feeling stuck and in need of a coach, a midwife to help me birth 15 Minutes of Grace. With pure humility and a twinkle in her eye she casually said, "I'm a writer. I can help you." My jaw dropped!

Then she looked at me deeper and said, "I WILL help You." Author Gwyn R.C. Moses, SHE hydrated me. A few weeks later we met in a local library. I felt every dream inside me leap. I was thinking, 'How does she just know? How does she SEE so deeply?'

Her counsel and wisdom were filled with so much mercy and light. When I left her, I felt like I was on a high. My excuses were not tolerated. She insisted my book would not be finished, until I yielded my will to the page, and release the pen to have its way. She drenched me with prayers, resuscitated my courage, then sent me on my way. I knew I had been given a precious gift that was greater than just her time and patience. SHE hydrated me.

Some time later after my book was published, I invited her to The Battle Station where we 'love everyday people, every day.' Her joy for me was sincere. Her laugh was infectious. Her stories mesmerizing and our spirits touched once again. The way she listens; to what you say and what you don't say. The way she's careful with her words. Like she knows her power. Everywhere she goes, she leaves love, and there is no doubt she has become Love. SHE hydrated me.

If your Soul is thirsty My Sister, Gwyn, sees You. She wrote these words with You in mind through the lens of her own experiences and conversations with God. Your dry and empty spaces are welcome here. Take a load off and dive into this Soulful experience with an open heart. I know from experience, her cup overflows and SHE has fully hydrated me.

Respectfully,
Sheila E. Battle
Author, 15 Minutes of Grace
TEDx RVA

Introduction

"Listen to life, and you will hear the voice of life crying, BE!" -James Freeman

'Supernatural embodiment of me is an autopsy of a tree. What a rising up! Distinct wholeness. Nature amends. She stands tall. Arms stretch wide in praise. Seasons are tucked inside. She thrives. Rebirths leaves of green multiplied. A search for a special tree leads me right back to me. It's in surrendering and letting it be. I see me free.'

I find myself walking, seeking, and communing among trees. Trees often lead to streams, ponds, lakes, and rivers. I am a river walker. Immerse myself with nature. I listen to hear the universe call. There is no other place I'd rather be to become one with nature, other than at a beach.

One quiet morning, Summer 2020, I woke up hearing, 'Fully Hydrated.' The voice spoke oh so sweetly. I immediately prepared myself for a day at the beach. I grabbed my paper and pen and headed to water. I had an urgency to hear, write, and expand how those two words would take form in meaning for me. From the unfolding, I present to the world SHE, Fully Hydrated.

Let's hope you, the reader, will be inspired to create a version of yourself that will be the you that you need. I recognize you in me. I believe this title erupted from my soul to reveal pitfalls and promises of my life have not overtaken me. I have felt life's rough tides and patiently waited beside still waters. I am still learning to be present in each moment to embrace the magic and specialness of it all.
SHE is me.

Sacred is SHE
She awakens at dawn
To the notes of birds
To richly satisfy him
She is of strength and dignity
The rule for what she does and says
Makes herself to be guarded
In beauty she is clothed
Sturdy hands
Thick thighs
Plump breasts
Wise with words
All she does is of goodness
She rejoices in celestrial light
She the giver of life
Energetic
Wholly

One night SHE stepped out of her dream.

She liked the way her feet hit the ground.
She liked how her hips swayed.
She liked the creative purpose felt
in her heart.

She liked her spirit, smile, and sanity.

She had the same unhappy thoughts
like most of you.

It took years to become stronger
and resilient.

She felt thirsty for laughs,
wisdom, joy, and generosity.

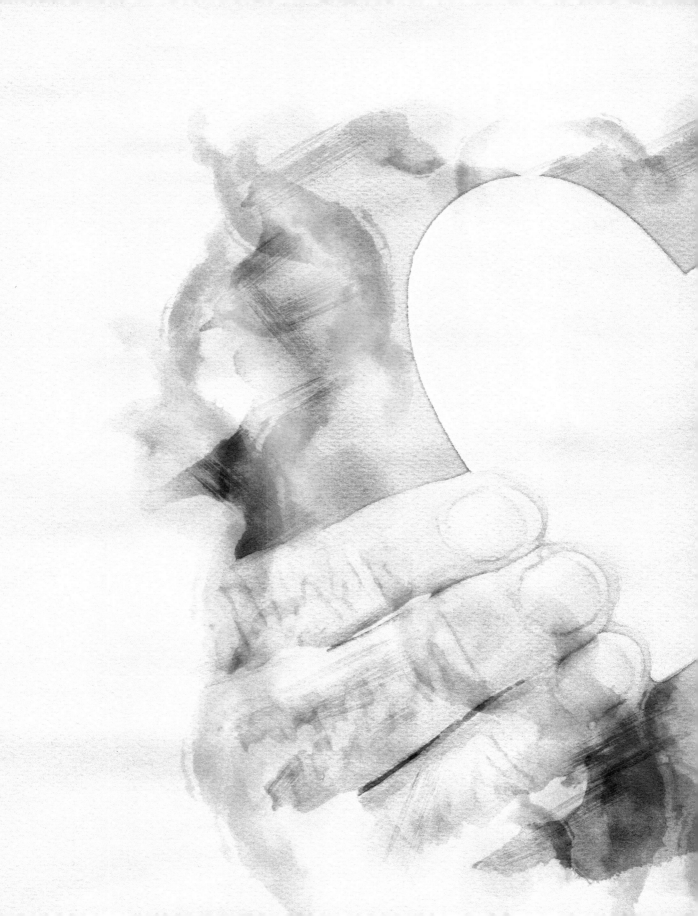

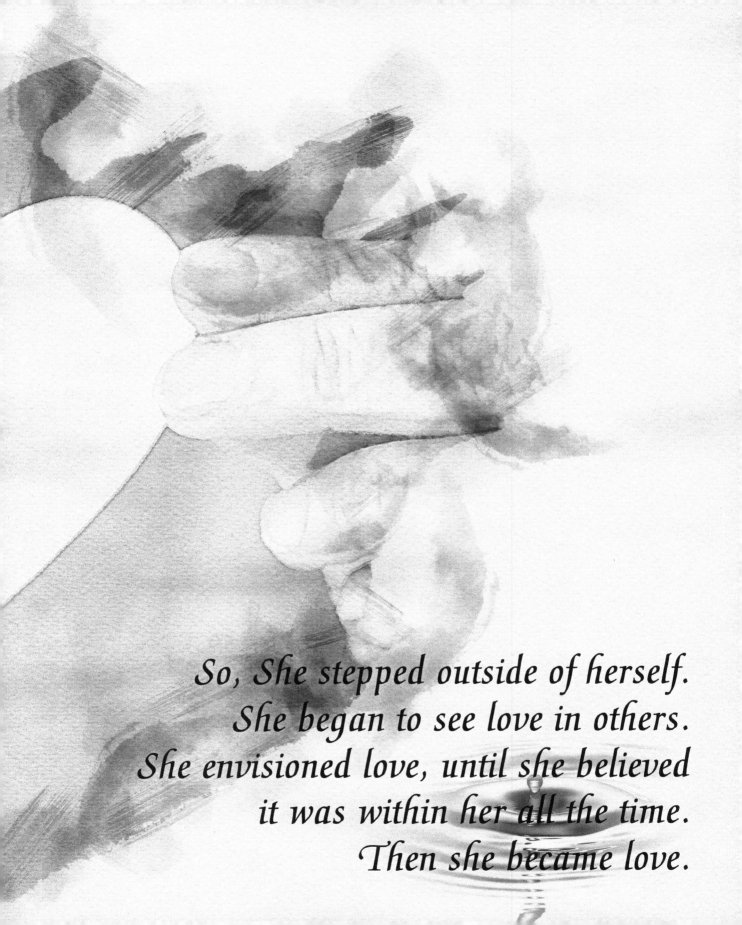

*So, She stepped outside of herself.
She began to see love in others.
She envisioned love, until she believed
it was within her all the time.
Then she became love.*

She realized she was enough.
She mattered.

She napped into the sunrise.
The sun rested upon her face as daily grace.

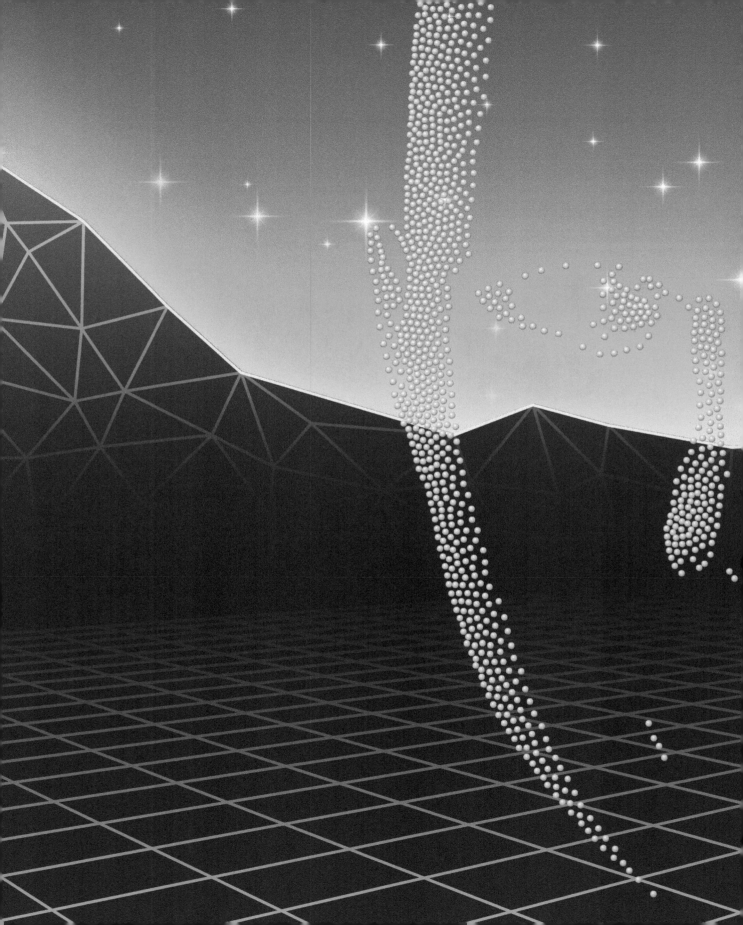

She made room for others.
She believed the world was too small.
She embraced magical moments.

She asked of the Universe to lead
and ran ahead even further.

She transformed foolish into wise.

She listened.
She forgave.
She knew she had to become her best self.

She stepped back into her dream.
She danced to the whistling of the wind.

She sat among trees.

She watched the branches
hold their heads down.

She heard leaves rustle with potential.

She triumphed through competitive seasons.

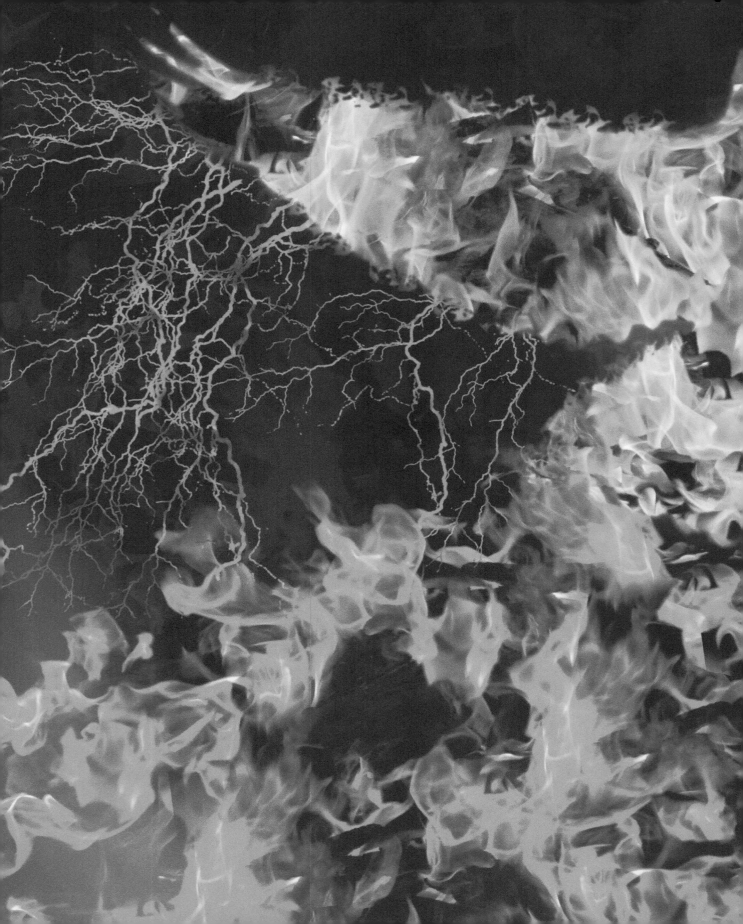

She embraced her strength.
She was bruised, but not broken.

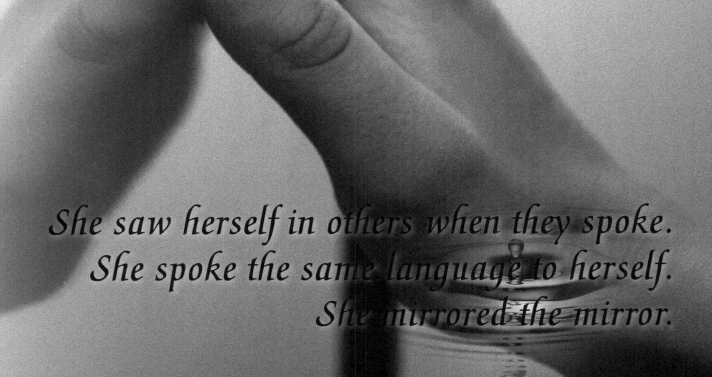

She saw herself in others when they spoke.
She spoke the same language to herself.
She mirrored the mirror.

Her secrets were held within her bosom.
She gave herself permission to choose.

She drank sweet wine, grew stronger,
became braver, and full of joy.

She opened her world to seeing everything as new.

Sacred is SHE.

SHE is me.